Kicking Goals: A Football Fan's Life with ALD

Kicking Goals: A Football Fan's Life with ALD

DANNY APPS

StoryTerrace

Text Danny Apps and Crystal Bennett, on behalf of StoryTerrace
Copyright © Danny Apps and StoryTerrace
Text is private and confidential

First print April 2024

www.StoryTerrace.com

This story is dedicated to the memory of my little brother Billy George Apps who I will love and miss forever

CONTENTS

CHAPTER 1: GROWING UP WITH MY BROTHER BILLY — 9

CHAPTER 2: LOSING MY BROTHER AND DEALING WITH ALD — 19

CHAPTER 3: ADJUSTING TO DISABILITY AT A NEW SCHOOL — 27

CHAPTER 4: BECOMING A SUPERFAN OF THE ARSENAL FOOTBALL CLUB — 33

CHAPTER 5: MY TRANSITION INTO ADULTHOOD - COLLEGE, JOBS AND NIGHTCLUBS — 43

CHAPTER 6: HOLLY - REKINDLING THE FLAME WITH THE LOVE OF MY LIFE — 49

CHAPTER 7: LIVING WITH A RARE DISORDER: MY ALD ACTIVISM — 55

CHAPTER 1: GROWING UP WITH MY BROTHER BILLY

I was born on July 25th, 1990 in London, England. I grew up in the area of Highams Park with my mum, dad, and younger brother Billy. We lived in Highams Park from the time I was around 3 years old until I was about 18 or 19 before moving to Woodford Green. Those were really happy times, especially the early years before my dear brother Billy got sick with a devastating disease called adrenoleukodystrophy (ALD).

Billy was my little brother, born three years after me. We were quite close despite fighting over things constantly as brothers do. We especially fought over football and video games, but at the end of the day, we loved each other deeply. Some of my earliest and fondest memories are of playing football with Billy in the local park or going head-to-head in video games on our PlayStation.

Even from a very young age, Billy was an excellent football player. He played goalkeeper and was so talented, even better than me! I was always in awe of his skill on the pitch. We would spend hours upon hours kicking the ball around together, often until our legs ached and our lungs burned. I was so proud to call him my brother.

When we weren't playing football, Billy and I could usually be found in front of the television battling it out with our favourite video games. We loved games like FIFA, racing games, adventure games - you name it! I still remember the competitive spirit between us during those sessions. We trash-talked each other and never let the other win easily. Despite how heated it would get sometimes, when the game was over, we'd laugh together and turn back into caring brothers.

Aside from sports and gaming, Billy and I did occasionally bicker and get on each other's nerves as brothers tend to do. We'd sometimes pick fights with each other just to get the other person in trouble. Our parents often had to break up squabbles between us. I'm ashamed to admit this now, but when we were very young, I once got so angry at him during a football match in the house that I accidentally pushed him into a glass window. It was a total accident borne out of frustration. Thankfully he wasn't badly injured, but I never forgave myself for losing control, even if just for a moment. All siblings have conflict, but we loved each other through it all.

During my early childhood, my mum worked exceptionally long hours to support our family. She worked at Sainsbury's supermarket and often left the house before dawn and didn't return until late in the evening. My dad didn't help out much with taking care of me and Billy while Mum was at work. Because both our parents worked such long hours, I have vivid memories of spending loads of time at my beloved nan's house with my little brother.

My nan lived in Ainslie Wood Road, very near to where we lived. Staying at Nan's house became a routine for Billy and me. Many mornings our mum would have us up and ready very early, sometimes when it was still dark outside. She'd take us to Nan's on her way to work. At Nan's we'd eat breakfast together, usually something delicious like bacon, eggs, and toast. After breakfast, Nan would look after us until it was time to walk to primary school just down the road. Those mornings spent in my nan's warm, cosy kitchen are some of my most treasured memories.

After school each day, Nan would be waiting to pick Billy and me up. We'd make the short walk back to her house again, where we'd spend the entire afternoon and evening. At Nan's, we felt free to just be boys, laughing, playing games, watching television, and snacking on sweets and crisps. Nan always had our favourite treats on hand. I have such fond recollections of those long days goofing around together at nan's house while our parents worked. My nan really stepped in and mothered us during those formative years.

When it was finally time for mum to finish work, she'd swing by Nan's to collect me and Billy and take us home. By that time of night, after a full day of school and playing, we were usually tired and ready for bed. Mum would get us bathed and into our pyjamas, and we'd zonk out the second our heads hit the pillows. Then the whole routine would begin again the next day.

I'm so thankful for the care my nan provided me and Billy when we were young. She gave us the attention, nurturing, and love we needed in our parents' absence. My nan was a remarkably kind, patient, and doting grandmother. She always had time to listen and chat with me. I hold those days very dearly in my heart, and I cherish the bond Billy and I formed during our childhood. We relied on each other when mum and dad were busy working. Billy was my best friend, despite our silly spats over football goals and high scores.

Sadly, my parents split up when I was in my early 20s and divorced in my mid 20s. That was a very difficult period in my adolescence. Thankfully the separation didn't become finalized until a few years later, but my parents' relationship was rocky all through my teens. I think they finally officially divorced around 2014 or 2015 when I was in my mid-20s.

It's never easy when my parents split up. In hindsight, I think both my mum and dad became much happier once they ended their marriage. They actually built an amazing friendship for quite a few years afterwards. Our family remained close, and there wasn't any of the bitterness you sometimes see. Still, adjusting to my parents living apart took time.

Little did I know that just a few short years later, our family would be devastated by a much greater tragedy - the loss of my beloved little brother Billy. The day my brother died remains etched in my memory and broke my heart in two. But I'll save that painful event for the next chapter. For now, I'm focusing on reminiscing on the cheerful, fun-filled days of childhood I shared with my best friend Billy. We had no idea what difficulties lay ahead for our family. I cherish those carefree early years and have learned to find joy in remembering Billy in his vibrant, mischievous youth before ALD darkened his life and ultimately took him away. More on that in Chapter 2.

My mum loved dressing me & Billy in the same outfits

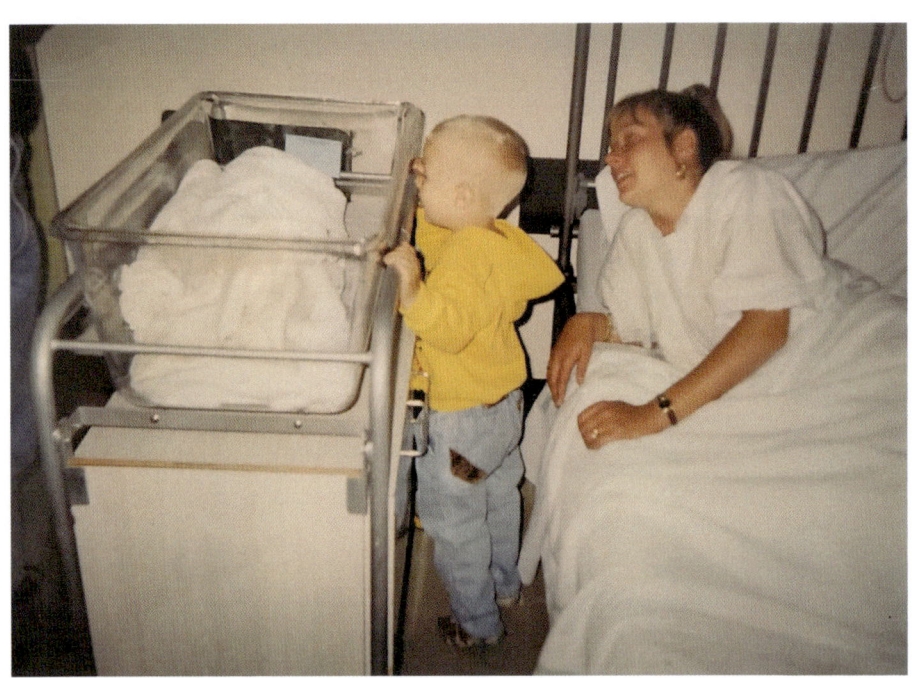
September 7th 1993 meeting my little brother Billy for the first time

My first day at Selwyn Infant school

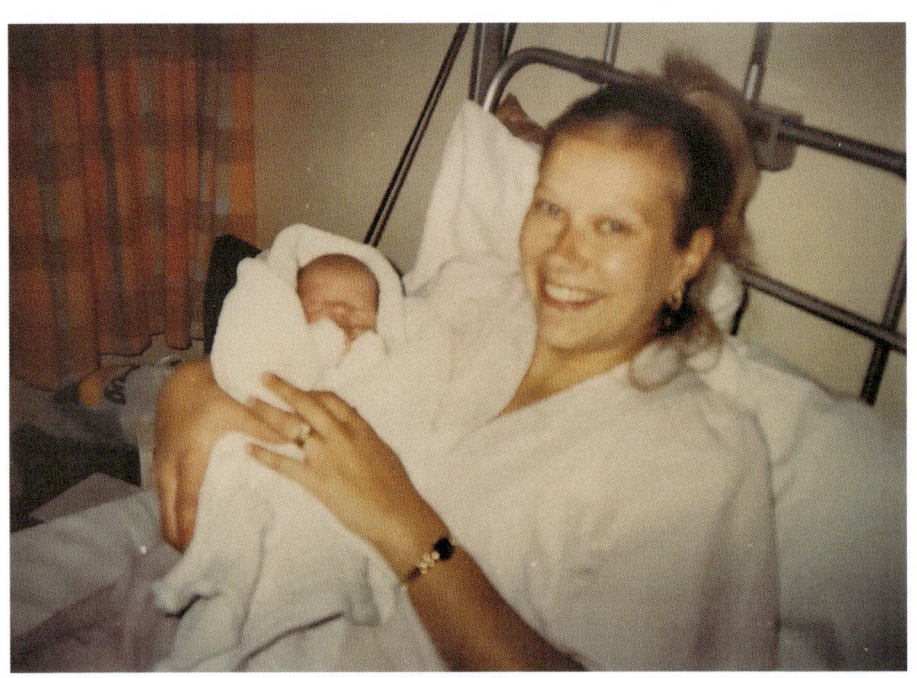

I was born on the 25th July 1990 just one day late

Celebrating my birthday in McDonald's with my friends the year before I was diagnosed with Adrenoleukodystrophy

CHAPTER 2: LOSING MY BROTHER AND DEALING WITH ALD

My childhood was happy and normal until I was 10 years old. That's when my world came crashing down in the blink of an eye. First, I lost my beloved younger brother Billy in 2000 when he passed away from a rare genetic disorder called adrenoleukodystrophy, or ALD. Then, just months later, I too was diagnosed with the same incurable condition that took my brother's life and would go on to take my eyesight and change the course of my life forever.

Billy was my little brother, just three years younger than me. We were so close growing up, even though we fought and teased each other all the time like brothers do. He was an amazing football player, I was so proud of his skills on the pitch. He played goalie and was always diving for spectacular saves. I was jealous of his talent but loved cheering him on.

When Billy was 6 years old, he was perfectly healthy and energetic. But shortly after turning 6, my mum started noticing some strange symptoms. Billy was walking on his tiptoes a lot and he started slurring his speech slightly. My mum took him to the doctor, thinking maybe he had just picked up a virus. But it turned out to be something far more serious. After many medical tests, Billy was diagnosed with ALD - adrenoleukodystrophy.

I didn't know anything about ALD at the time. Neither did my mum. It's a rare genetic disorder that damages the protective coating around nerve cells in the brain. Without this myelin sheath, the nerves can't properly send signals and eventually die off. ALD affects the nervous system and leads to problems with vision, hearing, speech, swallowing, adrenal function, and mobility. Back then, most people had never even heard of ALD. It was extremely rare.

The doctors told my mum that ALD is carried by women but normally only affects men and boys. Because my mum unknowingly carried the ALD gene, both her sons had inherited the disorder from her. Knowing what I know now about genetics, I don't blame my mum one bit. But at the time, finding out your two kids have an incurable illness that you passed on must have been earth-shattering for her.

After Billy's diagnosis, I was tested and found out I had ALD as well. But unlike Billy, I wasn't showing any outward symptoms yet. The doctors said that ALD normally emerges between ages 6 and 10 in boys, but each case can look different. For Billy, the ALD hit him fast and hard. Within just 10 months of being a perfectly healthy young boy, the ALD ravaged his nervous system and took his life. He passed away just four months after turning 7 years old.

Losing my little brother so quickly was completely devastating for me. One day we were laughing and playing football together, the next he was just...gone. My heart shattered into a million pieces at his funeral. I kept expecting him to walk through the door again, grinning that infectious grin of his. For months, I couldn't accept that I'd never see Billy again. We fought like cats and dogs, but I loved him so much. He was my little brother. We shared so many happy childhood memories of playing football in the park, taking care of our cat Scampi, or just joking around and teasing each other endlessly.

My mum tried to be strong for me, but I knew she was completely heartbroken too. She loved both her boys so much. At only 10 years old, I struggled to process losing Billy. I was confused, overwhelmed, distraught. I started sleeping with his photo under my pillow. I'd talk to him before bed every night. In my mind, he could still hear me. For a long time, it felt like there was a Billy-shaped hole in my heart that could never be filled. I missed him constantly. I still do, even all these years later.

While grieving such a profound loss, I also had to come to grips with my own ALD diagnosis. After losing Billy so tragically, the news that I also carried this incurable disease was frightening. I worried ALD was going to kill me too at any moment. I became anxious and depressed as a kid. My way of coping was detaching from my feelings, almost denying that I had ALD too. I tried to pretend everything was fine on the outside. But inside, I was terrified and confused about what my diagnosis meant.

In the months following Billy's death, my mum became consumed with researching everything she could about ALD. She connected with other families going through the same ordeal. She learned about experimental treatments like bone marrow transplants and a special oil called Lorenzo's Oil that might slow the progression of ALD. But there were no definitive answers or cures. All we could do was wait and see how the ALD would impact me.

Shortly before I turned 10 years old, I started noticing the first symptoms of ALD take hold - vision problems. I was sitting in my Year 5 classroom one day when I realized I couldn't see the chalkboard clearly anymore. The teacher's handwriting that had been crystal clear just days earlier now appeared blurred and illegible from my desk. I told my teacher that my eyesight seemed weird and blurry all of a sudden. She didn't believe me at first, thinking I was just mucking around as schoolboys do. But I insisted over and over that something was really wrong with my eyes.

Reluctantly, my teacher informed my mum about what I had told her. My mum immediately understood that my vision issues were likely the emergence of ALD, the same disease that took my brother. We went to the ophthalmologist and got the news we dreaded - the ALD was indeed beginning to damage my optic nerves and wreak havoc on my eyesight.

What followed was a painful couple of years of rapid vision loss during my final years of primary school. With each passing month, my sight grew exponentially worse. Simple tasks like reading the chalkboard or playing football became impossible. The world looked like an increasingly blurry impressionist painting. It was incredibly frustrating to go from perfect 20/20 vision one day to near blindness just a year or two later. My childhood slipped away from me.

By age 12, I had significant vision impairment. Just a short time earlier, I had been able to see everything clearly like any other kid. But ALD had swiftly robbed me of one of my most precious gifts - my sight. The rare genetic disorder that took my brother was now taking my vision too. It was utterly devastating, infuriating, and terrifying.

Yet despite the grim prognosis, my case of ALD has not followed the typical path. Most boys with ALD pass away at a young age, usually between 6 and 10 years old. So doctors see me and others like me who make it into our 20s and beyond as extremely unique cases, albeit still incurable. For reasons not fully understood, the ALD progressed only to a certain point and then seemed to stop its march of destruction in my nervous system. But the extensive damage to myelin can't be repaired.

Today, I'm in my 30s and living a full life. I rely on some adaptive technologies for reading, watching TV, and accessing information. I also have stiffness and mobility challenges due to the myelin sheath damage to my nerves. My legs don't function properly and I'm prone to falling down if I don't hold on to something or have my cane. But all things considered, I feel incredibly blessed to still be here and mostly stable so many years after my ALD diagnosis.

My journey with ALD has been a rollercoaster, full of devastating lows like losing my brother and my vision along with persevering through the highs and lows. I'm a survivor, plain and simple. I've overcome profound loss and disability all before my adulthood even began. It shaped me into a resilient, compassionate soul. While ALD took so much from me, it also gave me perspective and wisdom beyond my years. I don't sweat the small stuff because I know how precious life is and how quickly it can change.

Even all these years later, I think about my little brother Billy every single day. I close my eyes and cherish his memory in my mind. He's frozen in time as a smiling, athletic little 7-year-old boy who loved life and football. Losing him was the most painful experience of my life. It left scars on my heart that will never fully heal. Whenever I start feeling down or self-pity about my vision loss, I think of Billy and remember that I'm still here while his precious young life was cut so tragically short.

No child should have to endure what I went through at such a tender age. But adversity can also unlock true strength and resilience. My challenges with grief, disability and ALD taught me how to keep moving forward with determination and find my own path in life, however winding it may be. After all I've been through, I'm still here and still standing strong.

My life story took an unexpected turn that no one could have foreseen. Yet here I am, persevering despite everything. Some days it's still difficult to carry the weight of losing Billy and my vision. Some days ALD tries to pull me into sadness. But most days I'm able to find peace, joy and purpose in simple pleasures. I'm still me, just navigating the world a bit differently now. And Billy is always there beside me in spirit.

*There was over 500 people at my brothers funeral & this is just some of his flowers..
I called him Bruv*

CHAPTER 3: ADJUSTING TO DISABILITY AT A NEW SCHOOL

My eyesight started deteriorating fast when I was 10 years old. One day at school, I realized I could no longer see the chalkboard clearly. The teacher didn't believe me at first. But my vision got blurrier by the day.

That last year of primary school was so difficult. I struggled to see the board or my schoolwork. The school made no accommodations for my visual impairment. I felt frustrated and alone.

It became clear I could not continue mainstream education with my low vision. So at age 11, I transferred to a new school called Joseph Clark for blind and partially sighted students. I was very upset to leave my school and friends. But Joseph Clark ended up being the perfect place for me.

On my first day, I met my best friend Robert. We were in the same class and got along right away. Robert also had visual impairment. It was wonderful to have a real friend who understood my challenges.

Robert became my closest mate. We had such laughs together, playing pranks on teachers and chatting about girls we fancied. Our friendship made my difficult transition to special school smooth. I finally found my community, a place where I belonged.

All the teachers at Joseph Clark were amazing. Classes were tailored to our visual needs. We did touch-typing instead of handwriting, and had audio textbooks. Sports were adapted, like goalball instead of football. I never felt judged or pitied for my disability. The school celebrated what we could do, not what we couldn't.

I made so many friends at Joseph Clark. We had fun activities like art, drama and outings. I'll never forget our school trip to the seaside. For once, my visual impairment didn't hold me back.

Being around other students with low vision made me feel at home. I wasn't the only one dealing with sight loss anymore. Joseph Clark gave me a community who supported me through the difficult transition.

The school taught me vital skills for independence as a partially sighted person. I learned to travel safely and use assistive technology. My teachers gave me the confidence to navigate the world with low vision.

Attending Joseph Clark was hugely significant for my personal development. I found my place and came into my own. My disability was no longer something to be ashamed of, but part of what made me who I was.

After years of feeling isolated in mainstream school, I was finally accepted. Joseph Clark set me on the path to embracing my identity. I owe so much to the wonderful teachers and friends who made my years there so formative.

Leaving Joseph Clark was bittersweet. But it marked an exciting new chapter, which I'll discuss in the next part of my memoir. As a lifelong Arsenal football fan, I can't wait to share how I became a superfan and started going to games. But first, Joseph Clark gave me the strength to take on anything life threw my way.

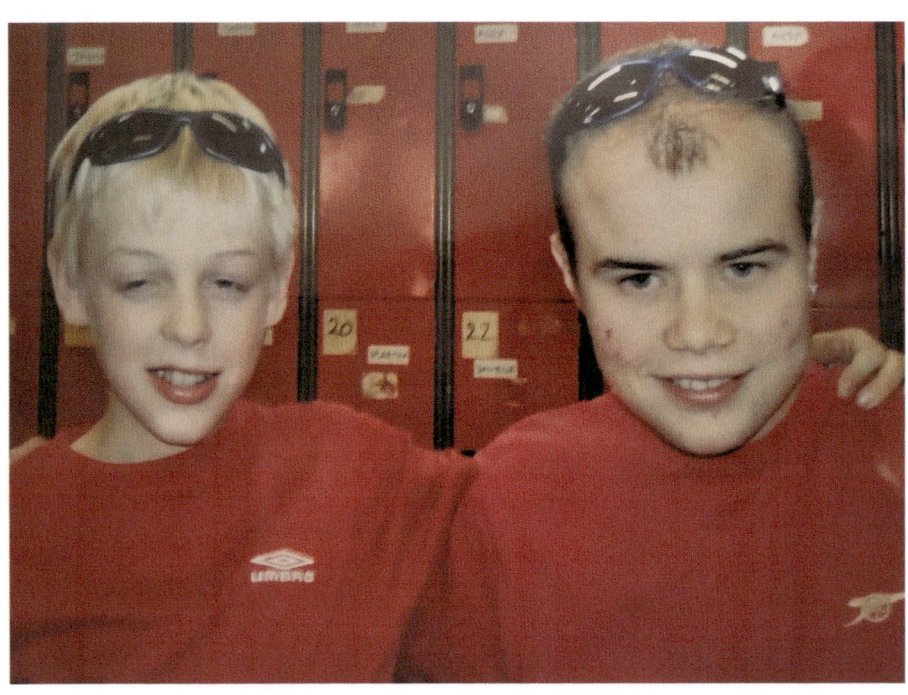

My friend Robert who is also visually impaired met him at Joseph Clarke school

Mr Reardon was my favourite teacher at Joseph Clarke school He used to make me laugh with his silly jokes

Sports day at Joseph Clarke school

CHAPTER 4: BECOMING A SUPERFAN OF THE ARSENAL FOOTBALL CLUB

Football has been my greatest passion since I was just six years old. I still remember the exhilaration of playing my first real match with other kids my age. My eyesight was perfect back then and I could run and kick and chase the ball with the boundless energy that only a young child possesses. Little did I know that in just a few short years, my ability to play would be cruelly snatched away from me by the progression of my illness, ALD. But my love affair with football has never wavered. Even once I couldn't play anymore, I found community and self-expression through religiously following my beloved club Arsenal. Now I'm a bonafide superfan who has been a season ticket holder for years.

My journey with football started when I was just entering primary school at age 6. Like most little boys in England, I was drawn to the beautiful game from the start. I'd kick a ball around with my brother Billy in our back garden and watch matches on TV, awestruck by the skill and passion of the players. My mum tells me I always had a football in my hands, even as a toddler. So it was only natural that I started playing for real with other kids once I was old enough.

KICKING GOALS: A FOOTBALL FAN'S LIFE WITH ALD

In those early days, I played locally for a few different youth clubs in the London area where I grew up. First was Ridgeway Rovers, where I proudly wore the number 8 shirt in honour of my childhood hero Ian Wright, Arsenal's legendary striker. I also played midfield and eventually striker for other teams including Grasshoppers and Wadham FC. I was totally obsessed with football back then. As soon as I came home from school, I'd beg my mum to take me to the park to play pick-up matches. Weekends were spent glued to the TV, taking in as much football as I could. And any chance I got, I'd practice drills and shoot at makeshift goals I constructed by turning over trash bins in our backyard.

Looking back, those were some of the happiest times of my young life. Playing actual matches with teammates my own age was an incredible feeling I'll never forget. My position on the pitch started out as a midfielder, but later I switched to striker where I really came into my own. I became quite a solid goal scorer thanks to my speed and scrappy style of play. My dream was to one day play professionally for a top Premier League club, hopefully, Arsenal. Sadly, that dream was cut short far too soon.

You see, from the time I was around 10 years old, my vision started deteriorating rapidly. This was a result of my illness ALD. This meant I was no longer able to play football competitively. My world collapsed because football was my life, my passion, my whole identity. I was heartbroken and depressed about having to quit the sport I loved.

Fortunately, while I could no longer play football, I could still passionately follow and support my team. Despite having to quit by age 10, my love for football has never gone away. If anything, it has grown even stronger over the subsequent years. I'm now a bonafide Arsenal FC superfan and avid student of the beautiful game.

My support for Arsenal stretches all the way back to my early childhood. When asked as a 6-year-old why I supported Arsenal, apparently I just said because they're the best. My brother was also a big Arsenal fan who idolized legendary players. So I guess supporting Arsenal just runs in my family. Initially, my mum was actually a Tottenham fan, but she wisely converted once she saw my brother and I had both pledged allegiance to the superior North London club.

Some of my earliest Arsenal memories are listening to matches on the radio with my dad and brother. We'd be practically levitating with excitement when Arsenal scored a goal. I also have fond memories of gathering around the TV with family to watch Arsenal knock their rivals. I was jumping and screaming so much I thought the neighbours would call the police on us! Those matches against their rivals cemented my status as a diehard, lifelong Gooner, as dedicated Arsenal supporters call themselves.

In 2001 when I was around 10 years old, I enjoyed one of the most thrilling experiences of my young life. My wonderful neighbour Bert, who knew of my passion for Arsenal, generously arranged for my family to get a VIP tour of Arsenal's training facilities. We also got to attend a real match at Arsenal's iconic home stadium on the same day. This was before Arsenal moved to their new stadium.

KICKING GOALS: A FOOTBALL FAN'S LIFE WITH ALD

Stepping inside Highbury and seeing a Premier League football match in person for the first time blew my mind. The atmosphere was absolutely electric. We had fantastic seats very close to the pitch. I'll never forget the spine-tingling feeling of hearing 38,419 fans belting out Arsenal's anthem at the top of their lungs. Seeing my heroes like Thierry Henry and Dennis Bergkamp playing live instead of on TV felt like a dream. I got to meet some of the star players after the match and get their autographs too. It remains one of the most euphoric experiences of my life all these years later. I knew then and there that I would be a lifelong Arsenal fan no matter what.

Attending that unforgettable match ignited an even more fervent passion for football within me. I started following Arsenal manically, learning everything I could about the players, the club's history, stats and league standings etc. I knew the starting 11 by heart and could recognise every player just by their silhouette or the way they ran. Going to Arsenal home matches became my favourite thing in the world. When Arsenal built their massive new stadium The Emirates in 2006, I became a season ticket holder the very first year it opened. I've kept the same seat for over 20 seasons now. I get it at a special discounted rate since I'm vision impaired.

Sitting in my seat surrounded by fellow diehard Arsenal fans makes me feel like I'm part of something bigger. The communal experience of cheering on our boys, riding the emotional highs and lows together, is just magical. Having a season ticket also means I get to meet Arsenal players face-to-face quite frequently when they do stadium tours or charity events. Over the years I've gotten autographs and photos with legends like Thierry Henry, Dennis Bergkamp and Ian Wright, though I sadly just missed the Bukayo Saka encounter. I've treasured those memories for life.

Nowadays since my mum can no longer accompany me to matches, her friends Dave and Angie have become my trusted match-day companions. They have been loyal friends who stepped up to take me to all of Arsenal's home and away matches, without fail. I feel so grateful to have people like them in my life who know how much football means to me and help me continue fueling my passion.

Attending Arsenal matches is still incredibly thrilling and entertaining for me after all these years. The atmosphere and pageantry of Premier League football never loses its lustre. I make sure to arrive hours early to soak up the pre-match atmosphere in and around the stadium. These days since my vision loss is so severe, I can't actually see the match action, unfortunately. But that doesn't dampen my enjoyment one bit! I have my own commentary box at The Emirates where I listen to live commentary and analysis through headphones. I know every player's style and can visualize the whole match in my mind. I've memorized the layout and visuals of The Emirates pitch so well from attending for years that watching the match unfold in my mind is still exhilarating. Sometimes I even fall asleep during matches because I'm so relaxed in my familiar surroundings! But the appeal never fades.

Football has essentially given me a sense of community, belonging and purpose throughout my life, despite all the hardships I've faced. My devotion to Arsenal has been a constant source of stability, excitement and joy ever since childhood. I'm so thankful that even though I had to stop playing early on, I've still been able to remain deeply involved as a passionate supporter. Being a football superfan gives me a clear identity and brings wonderful people into my life. I can't imagine existence without my beloved Arsenal FC! It's the greatest thing that ever happened to me aside from being born. I plan to keep attending matches and proselytizing the Arsenal gospel for the rest of my days on this Earth.

Just writing this has made me beyond excited for our next match...COYG (Come On You Gunners!) Now onto the next chapter, where I'll discuss my eventful transition into adulthood, including some wild times during my college days and nightclubbing adventures. But Arsenal will always remain my one true love.

Me & the last Arsenal manager Arsene Wenger. Met him twice once in 2001 & again in 2014

I was lucky enough to have a banner displayed outside the Emirates Stadium to celebrate Arsenal's 125 year Anniversary

Met the present Arsenal captain Martin Ødegaard in France 2023. First game abroad for me & they lost !!!

One of my alltime favourite Arsenal players the legend Thierry Henry

CHAPTER 5: MY TRANSITION INTO ADULTHOOD - COLLEGE, JOBS AND NIGHTCLUBS

After finishing school and getting diagnosed with adrenal leukodystrophy (ALD), I had to adjust to living with low vision in my late teens. Though challenging at times, this period of my young adult life also had many bright spots. I made some wonderful friends, gained more independence, and discovered brand-new passions and hobbies.

At age 16, I went to Waltham Forest College for four years and then went to Epping Forest College for another four years. The college offered special needs classes and assisted learning supports which were a huge help for me. In these classes, I met some of my closest friends—Sarah, Nicholas, Demi, Gemma and Holly. We had an instant connection and got up to all sorts of hilarious antics together. The teachers could barely keep us focused!

I have fond memories of pulling pranks on classmates, chatting endlessly about our favourite music and TV shows, and confessing our latest crushes. My friends brought out the best in me. For the first time, I felt like any other ordinary teenager, laughing and living it up with my crew.

Sarah and I grew especially close during our college years. We tried dating for a short time, but ultimately decided we were better off as friends. I was the one who introduced Sarah to her now longtime boyfriend, Nicholas. They are still together today and seem blissfully happy.

Though we have lost touch a bit since finishing college, I cherish the memories my friends gave me. We try to meet up a few times a year and relive the glory days over dinner. There is always lots of reminiscing and plenty of laughs when we reunite.

After completing college, I started attending a daycare activity centre for the visually impaired in 2021 when I was 31 years old. The centre provided important job skills training, as well as fun recreational activities like swimming, bowling, gardening and crafts. Though I enjoyed parts of the program, I was often bored by the limited activity choices. I am currently in the process of switching to a new daycare centre that offers more flexibility and independence.

In between daycare stints over the years, I have also held a few voluntary unpaid jobs thanks to the help of my support worker. One memorable role was working at a local charity shop. I assisted with sorting donations, pricing items, stocking shelves and serving customers. It was rewarding to try out a real workplace and gain experience. I hope to take on more employment in the future.

But my biggest hobby nowadays is undoubtedly going clubbing! This passion was born when I first went to a nightclub in my mid-20s, enjoyed it so much that I invited my best friend Sarah to come along. I absolutely fell in love with dancing the night away! The pulsing music, the laughter of friends, and the carefree atmosphere were like nothing I had experienced before.

After that first hesitant visit, I became a regular clubgoer almost immediately. These days, you can find me at Club@82's infamous "Lost in Music" night once a month. I only missed going once in the six years since they launched this event. There is always a different fun theme, from Halloween to Valentine's Day. I dress up in costume with my friends, hit the dance floor, and don't leave until they kick us out at closing!

Over the years, I've gotten to know the warm and welcoming Club@82 staff. The lively music and reasonably priced drinks don't hurt either. Going clubbing has become my ultimate outlet for letting loose. When I'm dancing out on that checkered floor, nothing else matters except living in the moment.

My college days and newfound clubbing hobby marked the transition into adulthood. I became more confident and independent from my family. Though still close with my mother, I branched out socially and pursued my own interests. This was an important period of personal growth for me.

The next chapter will recount my journey to find love and reconnect with a cherished ex-girlfriend named Holly. Though we had a painful breakup, the flame between us never fully died. Get ready for a story of persistence, forgiveness, and second chances.

My teachers & fellow students at Waltham Forest college

Receiving a certificate at Epping college

My best friend Sarah who I met at Epping college

CHAPTER 6: HOLLY - REKINDLING THE FLAME WITH THE LOVE OF MY LIFE

Like many people my age, relationships are incredibly meaningful in my life. My mental health often struggles when I'm single for too long. I've learned through experience that my ex-girlfriend Holly is the perfect romantic partner for me - we just 'get' each other in a way no one else does. Now, with the support of our families, we might be able to pick up where we left off years ago and finally have the beautiful relationship we've always dreamed of.

I've had a few girlfriends over the years, but I often struggle with low self-worth when I'm not in a relationship. My self-confidence takes a big hit whenever I'm single for an extended period. Though my close friends and family remind me of my positive qualities, it's just not the same as having that special someone who understands and connects with me on a deeper level.

Without question, the most meaningful relationship I've had so far was with my ex-girlfriend Holly, who also happens to have additional needs. We truly understood each other and consistently lifted each other up with compassion. Holly struggled with depression, so I did my best to make her laugh and feel cared for whenever we were together. In return, she showered me with affection and made me feel like the luckiest guy in the world.

Holly and I shared so many common interests, which made our time together effortless and fun. We were both huge animal lovers - she had a cat who got along great with my terrier Bob. We came from similar family backgrounds and even grew up in the same part of town. Our musical tastes aligned perfectly - we'd listen to pop songs from the 2000s for hours in my room.

My amazing mum, who was so happy to see me in a healthy relationship, often took me and Holly out for meals on the weekend. Mum was basically our free taxi service, driving us anywhere we wanted to go! One time, I even took Holly with me to an Arsenal football game. She came along primarily to spend time with me, even though she actually supported West Ham.

After over a year of dating blissfully, Holly's overprotective twin brother decided he didn't approve of our relationship. He believed I was 'taking his sister away' from him by me and Holly spending so much time together. Despite my efforts to bond with him, he turned Holly against me by constantly putting me down. He'd tell her terrible lies about me 'mistreating' her, none of which were remotely true.

Her brother's meddling meant Holly eventually ended our relationship, even though we were totally in love and committed to each other. I was emotionally crushed when she left me and descended into a deep depression. For months, I moped around heartbroken, desperately trying to win her back. But Holly had been too badly influenced by her brother's cruel lies.

In the years after losing Holly, I tried dating other people but never got over her. She was my confidant, my cheerleader, my soulmate - and I'd lost her. No matter who I temporarily dated next, I'd inevitably compare them to Holly in my mind. Nobody could compare to the blissful connection we'd shared.

Then, a few months ago, I bumped into Holly completely by chance on a night out. The intense sparks between us reignited instantly. We laughed, hugged, and promised to meet up again soon. My mum and Holly's mum remembered all the joy and stability I'd brought to Holly's life in the past. My mum agreed to support us if we gave the relationship another chance, but Holly's mum wants us to just be friends for the time being.

After our serendipitous reunion, I learned Holly has really struggled with worsening depression over the past few years. She could genuinely use my help to get through this exceedingly tough period in her life. I want nothing more than to be by her side, making her smile every day like I used to.

Holly's brother Ryan will not sway me this time. Our unbreakable bond and mutual devotion far outweighs anything he might try to sabotage. I intend to stand up to Ryan, letting him know his interference will no longer be tolerated. Holly and I deserve a fighting chance at the beautiful relationship we've dreamed of for so long.

My wonderful mum is overjoyed at the thought of me getting back with Holly. She remembers how perfectly we complimented each other and thinks we're destined to be together. Holly's mum obviously wants us to take things slow and just be good friends for now. But I know she appreciates how much I adore her daughter, so hopefully she'll come around in time.

I often daydream about the amazing day when my best friend, confidant and soulmate Holly finally moves in with me permanently. We'll spend our time playing with our dogs, going to Arsenal matches, and supporting each other through any mental health struggles. My bond with Holly has proven unbreakable - our time apart has only made me love and appreciate her even more. With persistence and communication, I believe we can move past the pain of the past. This time, nothing will tear us apart.

Me & my lovely Holly having lunch in Pizza Express

CHAPTER 7: LIVING WITH A RARE DISORDER: MY ALD ACTIVISM

My brother Billy and I were both born with a rare genetic disorder called adrenoleukodystrophy, or ALD for short. This condition damages the protective myelin sheath that covers nerve cells in the brain, gradually leading to neurological impairments. Most boys with ALD tragically pass away in childhood, but against the odds, I have lived with it for over 20 years as a long-term survivor. This life-altering diagnosis has shaped my identity and disability experience profoundly. Now as an advocate for greater ALD awareness, I want to share my story to help other families facing this devastating disorder.

When my brother and I were diagnosed, my poor mum had no prior knowledge that she carried the ALD gene. This genetic mutation is passed from mother to son, lying dormant and impossible to detect unless explicitly tested for. I was 10 years old when the first symptoms appeared, while Billy was only 6. It began with subtle changes like Billy walking on his tiptoes, then progressed to slurred speech and loss of coordination. My mum brought Billy to the doctor, alarmed something was seriously wrong with her young son. After various tests, we received the devastating news that Billy had ALD. Further testing also confirmed that I had inherited

ALD as well. This rare disorder affects only 1 in 20,000 people, and few had even heard of it at the time.

Initially, I seemed less impacted than Billy, still able to play football and attend mainstream school. But around age 10, I started experiencing vision problems looking at the chalkboard in class. My sight progressively deteriorated over the next few years due to ALD, ultimately leaving me legally blind. Beyond vision loss, ALD also gradually stiffened my legs and impaired balance and mobility. I rely on a cane for stability and have difficulty navigating new environments. But thankfully my upper body remains unaffected, allowing me to independently perform self-care and household activities.

After diagnosis, we urgently tried medical interventions to slow the rapid neurological degeneration. ALD patients lack an enzyme to process certain fats, allowing these to build up in the brain and damage myelin. We started on Lorenzo's Oil, a mixture of oils that attempted to block this fat accumulation. But tragically, this experimental treatment failed to halt my brother's swift decline. Billy passed away only 8 months after diagnosis, robbing him of the chance to really experience life. Losing my best friend and football teammate at only age 7 devastated me. I was angry that ALD stole my dear brother away, angry at the universe for this cruel injustice.

In those early terrifying years after Billy's death, the unpredictability and genetic aspect compounded the trauma of ALD. We had no way to anticipate how rapidly my condition might advance or what symptoms could develop. The diagnosis also implicated my mother - she unknowingly passed this genetic mutation down to her two sons. But of course, she carries no blame. The genetic counsellors comforted my mum that without explicit testing, there was simply no way she could have known. But ALD introduced fear and fragility into our family, including uncertainty about what the future held for me.

Against the typical prognosis, I have lived over 20 years with stable ALD symptoms. Around age 20, we confirmed via brain imaging that the ALD progression had remarkably halted on its own. My doctors could not explain my unexpected longevity and plateau of symptoms. We dubbed me and another young man "miracle boys", who both oddly escaped the fate expected with this disorder. After over a decade of tolerating the awful taste and side effects of Lorenzo's Oil, I recently chose to stop this ineffective medication under the doctor's supervision. But we continue monitoring my ALD status closely with regular neurological evaluations and scans for any changes. I hope and pray each time that my scans come back stable.

Having survived this adversary, I now devote myself to raising awareness about adrenoleukodystrophy. The lack of knowledge regarding ALD compounded the stress and isolation my family experienced. I share my story to spread understanding of this rare disorder, working to put ALD "on the map" in even a small way. I have participated in genetic research studies and now published this biography detailing my unique medical journey. Each time I speak out, I gain confidence as a self-advocate and activist.

KICKING GOALS: A FOOTBALL FAN'S LIFE WITH ALD

The ALD community weekends are organised by a charity called Alex TLC. The charity was set up by the mum of two brothers who also had ALD. Sadly her eldest son Alex (whom the charity is named after) also passed away from this disease.

Attending hospital ALD meetings allowed me to connect with fellow patients. But our experiences vary widely based on factors doctors cannot yet predict. I clung to the hope that a miracle bone marrow transplant could save my life as it does for some. But emerging research suggests this risky procedure cannot help ALD patients like myself with ongoing myelin damage. Treatment advances remain slow coming for this rare disorder. My neurologist says I am one of the oldest living ALD survivors she has encountered. Each extra year grants me precious time to embrace life's joys and make lasting memories with loved ones.

In many ways, I aim to live my life to the fullest while my health permits, travelling abroad and pursuing hobbies like gaming and dance. ALD requires me to accept support from family who assist with household tasks and transport. But I still exercise fierce independence navigating the world as safely as possible. Some days, the leg stiffness and mobility challenges frustrate me deeply. My football dreams ended prematurely when those symptoms emerged at age 10. But focusing on my abilities, not limitations, helps me maintain a positive attitude. I cannot know what the future holds concerning my ALD prognosis. For now, I celebrate each milestone, birthday and accomplishment. My disorder does not define me - I define myself through my character and achievements.

KICKING GOALS: A FOOTBALL FAN'S LIFE WITH ALD

The grief over losing Billy permeates our family, and I carry my dear brother in my heart each day. As long as I persist in this world, I honour Billy's memory through activism and outreach. My mission is forging a greater understanding of ALD's impacts on patients and caregivers. This path brings me solace, purpose and courage. Though ALD cannot be outrun indefinitely, I keep surpassing expectations thanks to milestone treatments, supportive care and probable genetic luck. I urge families facing new ALD diagnoses to remember - hope always remains. Patients can exceed their prognosis with access to dedicated healthcare specialists, thorough monitoring and emerging therapeutics.

Progress happens, even if agonizingly incremental. As an ALD advocate, my voice joins the chorus demanding expanded research and clinical trials for rare disorders often overlooked. My story undeniably contains great sorrow and hardship. But I write to inspire others experiencing a perception of "life limits" imposed by illness or disability. With tenacity and support from loved ones, horizons expand in unexpected ways. Life continually unfolds if you keep the faith.

Just as football matches ebb and flow, my health status has risen and fallen throughout my 33 years of living with adrenoleukodystrophy. I weather rough tackles from this disorder much like a goalkeeper blocking powerful shots on goal. Some slip past my defences, like sudden vision loss derailing my football career. But many others I successfully deflect, surviving decades now with ALD. My devoted fans -

my mum, aunties, cousins, Dave and Angie at matches - cheer me on in this match that extends across a lifetime.

Of course, the ultimate victory against ALD remains elusive - steady research progress but no cure just yet. I often grow impatient waiting to convert a decisive penalty kick, ready to claim triumph over ALD. My soul longs to break free and score that final winning goal. Yet the game clock ticks on. Until that glorious moment arrives, I hustle relentlessly across the field. Skirmishes arise but my steadfast perseverance stays the course.

My indomitable spirit knows no fatigue or fear. I surge forward to seize not just survival, but joy and purpose. The stands roar approval, loving supporters instilling faith to stay brave in adversity and savour each moment's gifts. No illness or condition circumscribes my worth. With the encouragement of family and friends, I can achieve anything. Eyes fixed on the prize, I am an ALD warrior, constantly advancing the ball toward hope's goal line. The final buzzer will sound only when research yields a cure restoring lives interrupted by this disease. Until then, the competition remains in play. And I am ever ready for victory's next shot.

My last Christmas with both my nan & Grandad

Met Shaun (who also has Adrenoleukodystrophy (ALD) at the first community weekend for boys & family with ALD

The football team my uncle played for raised funds so I could go to Florida this is me kissing Natalie the dolphin

StoryTerrace

Printed in Great Britain
by Amazon